It's Your
Decision

7 Key Decisions To
Leading a More Rewarding Life

DR. MILTON MATTOX

Published in the United States of America

ISBN 978-1-7359755-0-4

Synergy Biblio Publishers
3104 E Camelback Road #2040
Phoenix, AZ 85016
inquiry@synergybiblio.com
www.synergybiblio.com

First Edition

Disclaimer

The information in this book is true and complete to the best of the author's and publisher's knowledge. Any advice or recommendations are made without guarantee on the part of the author or publisher. Some of the key decisions listed in this book were conceptualized prior to the current COVID-19 pandemic. Readers should refer to the guidelines from the Centers for Disease Control and Prevention (CDC), and the World Health Organization (WHO) during these pandemic times. The author and publisher disclaim any liability in connection with the use of this information.

All characters and other entities appearing in the Introduction of this book are fictitious. Any resemblance to real persons, *dead or alive*, or other real-life entities, *past or present*, is purely coincidental.

Dedication

To my mother and father,

Though you are both with our Lord and Savior, your teachings continue to guide me every day of my life. If it is His will, I seek to pass on some of the lessons you taught me via the words written down in this book.

Table of Contents

Introduction

The end result of your life here on earth will always be the sum total of the choices you made while you were here.

–Shad Helmstetter

Imagine if you will, Chloe and Alyssa, identical twin girls separated at birth. Both were adopted into similar homes, had loving parents, grew up in nice neighborhoods, and attended great schools. They both knew they were adopted, but didn't know that they had an identical, biological twin somewhere in the world. Even though they didn't grow up together, they had many similar personality traits.

Right after high school graduation, Chloe's adopted father died suddenly of a massive heart attack. She and her father had been very close, and his death affected her deeply. She was so overwhelmed with grief that she felt she couldn't start college as planned. What started off as only deferring school for a few months, turned into continuing to live at home with her mother for the next couple of years, and having to find odd jobs. Though her mother tried to persuade her to continue her education, Chloe felt defeated and didn't see any benefit to going back to school. It had always been her father's dream to watch his little girl walk the big stage and receive her degree, but since he wouldn't be there, she couldn't face it; it just wouldn't be the same without him.

Over the next few years, she watched many of her friends graduate from college, some of them even achieving advanced degrees and becoming successful doctors, lawyers, teachers, writers and engineers. She observed their victories in silent and sometimes bitter envy, as she continued her struggle to barely earn a minimum wage. Most employers, she found, would much rather hire skilled laborers and educated workers for the same jobs she sought.

One day while in between jobs, Chloe attended a free seminar at the local library. She had heard it would be led by a young university professor who was a recognized expert in her field. She barely heard any of the lectures because she was so distracted by an apparent mirror image of herself onstage who confidently commanded the spotlight. When the last speaker had finished and people began to file out, Chloe gathered the courage to approach her doppelgänger, and it was like having a conversation with a more polished, successful version of herself.

Both intrigued by their uncanny resemblance, they sat and talked for a long time afterward, and quickly discovered that they were long-lost twins. The incredible joy and excitement of finding each other after nearly twenty-seven years was overwhelming. They cried, laughed, and hugged, and then cried, laughed, and hugged some more.

Chloe and Alyssa got together for lunch the next day and talked about everything from their childhoods to the present, and everything in between. They marveled at the unbelievable similar turns their lives had taken, including the loss of a parent shortly after high school graduation. Beyond that, however, the similarities ended.

They realized that the biggest difference between them stemmed back to the decisions made following their parent's death. Alyssa had been highly influenced by the positive affirmation and personal growth books she had devoured from a young age. When her mother died, she had a choice to make; she could wallow in the grief of her mother's death forever, or she could celebrate her mother's life by following in her footsteps to obtain a college degree. She chose the path her mother would have been proud of and went on to get her college degree, as well as master's and doctorate degrees in mathematics.

When Chloe's father died, she, too, had a choice to make. Her choice, however, had led her down a path of depression and stagnation. Prior to their loss of a parent, the twins had led near-identical lives.

Chloe confessed to Alyssa how disappointed she was in herself for not living up to her potential. She was heartbroken for having let her father down and not pursuing an education and a future like he had wanted for her. She told Alyssa how happy she was for her success, about how dissatisfied she was with her own life, how she wished she could turn back time and do things differently.

Alyssa was quiet for a moment, but then she looked at her sister with the biggest, brightest smile and said, "Happiness is not determined by your situation. Your state of happiness is determined by you." She gently reminded Chloe that she was still young, and still had a long life ahead of her. She encouraged her not to dwell on the past, because the future is as bright as she wants it to be. She said, "Decide what you want your future to be right now, and take small steps every day to reach that goal."

Chloe decided to make the right choice this time. She took her sister's advice to heart and enrolled in the local university. Over the following four years, she worked tirelessly to obtain her college degree, then went on to earn her master's and doctorate degrees in history. She became a published author of mystery novels, has several bestsellers to her name, and now she knows that whatever she wants in life is only a choice away.

Life's Choices

While the story you just read is fictional, it serves as a great example of the impact of the choices we make in life. The intent of the story is to show life's parallels stemming from the choices we make. One choice led to a mediocre life for one of the twins in the story, while making a different choice under a similar circumstance gave the other twin a life of prestige and professional accomplishment.

The obvious point is that, had the one twin living a mediocre life made a different decision following the death of her father, she too could have had a life blessed with success instead of struggle. More importantly, the moral of the story is that it's never too late to make new choices and forge a better, more positive path through life.

It Really Is That Easy

You've probably often heard the sayings "that's easier said than done" or "that's not so easy." People tend to be creatures of habit and will often stick to what they know even if they're not happy because it's easier to do nothing than it is to change. They'll argue that deciding to change your life is the easy part; actually doing it is what's difficult. Although it's true that changing one's life can definitely have its challenges, the decision to start isn't so difficult. In other words, it *is* that easy, if you want it to be.

The keys to making a decision and changing your life for the better include the following high-level steps:

1. Decide to do something different in your life.

2. Visualize your desired goal.

3. Believe that you can turn your goals into reality.

4. Identify and take small steps leading toward your visualized goal every day.

5. Celebrate after each accomplished step.

As you can see, you start by making a **decision**. An example might be that you have always wanted to write a book, so you decide that you will be an author. At this stage, don't worry about how long it will take or the detailed steps involved. Your only thought at this step is that you have decided to become an author and write a book.

The next step is to **visualize** and imagine yourself as a published author. In your mind, you think about your book in the finished state, you might even picture your book's cover with your name on it. You can see it selling in hardcover, paperback, and electronic format wherever books are sold. You picture yourself signing copies of the book for your family, friends, colleagues, and even strangers. In your mind, the book is already written and published. Again, at this stage, you are not concerned about exactly how you will reach this point. It's important to create a visual for yourself, as vividly as possible, of achieving that which you desire. You will repeat this visualization exercise every day until you've reached your goal.

Next, you need to **believe** that you will achieve your goal. This is a very important step, because if you don't believe it, then you're setting yourself up for failure. Life is full of naysayers, and people will try to dissuade you. People you love and respect will tell you it's not going to work, and that you'll never reach your goal. They'll remind you how you know nothing about writing a book, and how difficult it is. Don't listen to them; the only thing that matters is what *you* believe.

Once you believe you can and will achieve the goal, and no one other than yourself can deter you from reaching it, the next step is to identify small steps that will help you get there. Once you've identified and listed all the steps leading toward your goal, make sure that you take at least one of these steps every single day. If you happen to miss a day or two, that's okay; remind yourself that you're human and give yourself a little grace. Then just pick up where you left off and keep going. In keeping with the example of becoming an author, you may decide one of your steps is that every day, you will write at least one sentence, paragraph, page, or chapter – no matter what. You will find that some days the words flow like water and you will easily write a chapter. Other days, you might barely muster a single sentence, and that's fine. Whether you write a sentence or a chapter, you will be one small step closer to achieving your goal at the end of each day.

The last step is just as important as the others, and that is to celebrate the achievement of your steps. You may celebrate at the completion of each chapter by going out to dinner with friends, or maybe all you want is to give yourself a day off from writing to just reflect on the progress you have made. No matter how you choose to celebrate, the important thing is that the reward is something that is meaningful to you.

Follow these steps, and before you know it, you will have reached your goal. Use them to achieve almost any goal, your imagination is your only limit. Remember that the first step is the most important; you must start by making a decision. No matter what your current life situation is, the decision to achieve most, if not all, of your goals is still absolutely yours to make.

Overview

Over the years, I have found that there are seven key decisions that can help you live a much more rewarding and positive life. You have to decide to do each of the seven things before you can reap the rewards of the decision. The seven decisions are as follows:

- Decide that love is one of humankind's greatest gifts – don't be afraid to love.

- Decide to be happy – right now.

- Decide that "it" is easy – not hard.

- Decide to hug someone today – you'll make their day.

- Decide to genuinely listen to people more often than you speak.

- Decide to be healthy starting right now.

- Decide to be the person you want to be, and be that person – starting right now.

The details of the seven decisions listed above are covered in chapters one through seven. Each of the seven chapters has the following high-level structure:

- Opening Discussion

- Historical Perspective

- The Decision in Action

- Practical Ways to Implement the Decision

- Takeaways

Specifically, each chapter begins with a discussion about the decision to set the context. I then review the history of the main subject of the decision. For example, the first decision is about love, so the etymology of the word *love* is reviewed, along with the overall historical perspective of how great leaders and public figures have implemented the decision in the past. Afterward, I take a look at the decision in action where the decision is being used to affect positive change in one's life. I then briefly identify practical ways in which the decision can be implemented, followed by a few important takeaways from the discussion.

The last two chapters include a discussion about how to put all the decisions into action, and concluding thoughts. Once you have finished reading the book, it is my sincerest hope that you will understand and believe that it is truly your decision to determine your state of well-being, no matter your age or your current situation in life. Your state of well-being is a relative situation, not a comparative one. If you spend your life comparing yourself to others, then you may feel that you don't have a choice. However, if you focus on the things that are relative to you, then you will find that your state of well-being really is your decision and that ultimately it is you who is in control of your own happiness.

Call to Action

At the end of the book, you'll find a convenient section you can use as your own personal journal. A place to write down your decisions, steps, and victories on your journey to a happier life. There is also a web address directing you to the same resource online. This was mainly implemented for those of you who have purchased the electronic version of this book, however, it's available to everybody.

Chapter 1

Decide That Love Is One of Humankind's Greatest Gifts – Don't Be Afraid to Love

"Love your neighbor as you love yourself."

-Mark 12:31

Opening Discussion

One of the most wonderful yet enigmatic gifts to humankind is love. If we all had unconditional love for each other, the world would truly be a better place. I'm not referring to sexual or narcissistic love; I'm referring to the kind of love where mutually shared respect, support, and trust among all people abound. It is important that love be unconditional as well, because if love is given only because it is expected in return, then the true power of love will not come to fruition.

Love is an enigma because the secret to the survival of humankind is love, yet we choose not to use it unconditionally. Logically, if everyone loved one another, the world would be a better place, however, many of us choose to only love those who are like us. While it seems impossible that everyone in the world would suddenly start to love each other unconditionally, you can begin unraveling the mystery of love by making the decision to love unconditionally starting right now. This will have a positive impact on the people around you as love is infectious, especially when it is available in abundant supply.

Love is the greatest gift given by God to all humanity. The concept of love is the crux of most major religions. Love is at the heart of the universal Golden Rule (or the Ethic of Reciprocity) maxim where we should treat each other as we wish to be treated. In Christianity, Jesus commands us to love our neighbor as we love ourselves. The first part of this command is the challenge to love oneself first; you can only love your neighbor to the measure you love yourself. No one can love you more than you love yourself. Loving yourself must be the core of your entire being. True self-love is the very foundation of wellbeing, joy, self-empowerment, and your ability to create and enjoy the kind of life you desire. You cannot enjoy true happiness if you are not at peace with yourself; your relationship with yourself is the most important one you'll ever have.

The Judaic-Christian Bible states that our ability to love and accept the gift of love comes from our relationship with Jesus Christ. "*We love because He first loved us" (1 John 4:19).* We are able to love because Jesus loves us. Love is something that is passed from one person to another;

it doesn't exist in a vacuum. The ability to give and receive love is the greatest gift of all. God made us in His image, because of His love. Love needs an outlet and yearns to be expressed and shared with others. It is because we are created in His image that we have the innate ability to love one another, just as He loves each of us.

Historical Perspective

The word 'love,' originally spelled 'leubh,' has been used for over five thousand years to describe care and desire. The word can be traced back to the Indo-European culture and has given birth to a huge lexical progeny. Love is used to describe one of the most powerful experiences available to all humans. When love was incorporated into Old English, as 'lufu,' it became both a noun describing deep affection and a verb pertaining to fondness.

One of the earliest recorded uses of the word 'love,' and perhaps its largest influence, is the Judaic-Christian Bible. It was used to describe both the benevolence and affection of God towards humans and the affectionate devotion due to God. From the 1611 King James Bible, *"God is love, and he that dwelleth in love, dwelleth in God."* (John 4:16). From this widely recognized meaning, love began to be used to positively describe instances of affection or acts of kindness.

"Hatred paralyzes life; love releases it. Hatred confuses life; love harmonizes it. Hatred darkens life; love illuminates it." Dr. Martin Luther King, Jr.'s words are a timeless example of the power of love. His volume of sermons entitled *Strength to Love* first published in 1963, continues to promote his vision of love as a potent social and political vehicle for change. This seminal work holds the idea that love, something the world likes to view as weak and passive, can have a powerful impact. We can draw inspiration and strength from people such as Dr. Martin Luther King, Jr., Gandhi, and Nelson Mandela. Each of them a peaceful leader who changed the world with love, whose messages of love prevail even to this day.

Deciding that love is one of humankind's greatest gifts can be one of the most important and life-altering decisions you will ever make. Start by providing unconditional love to the people around you. Not everyone will be receptive to this approach, and some will question your motives. Most people, however, will welcome your newfound perspective with joy. It's your decision; decide that love is a gift, and start providing unconditional love today.

The Decision in Action

Throughout her lifetime, Mother Teresa received numerous awards, including the Nobel Peace Prize in 1979. She spent a lifetime living out Jesus' love; selflessly helping the poor, the dying, and those in need in Kolkata, India. Mother Teresa sums up her feelings, saying, "We have all been created for greater things; to love a person, without any conditions, without any expectations. Works of love are works of peace and purity. Works of love are always a means of becoming closer to God, so the more we help each other, the more we love God better by loving each other." Another quote by Mother Teresa states, "It is not how much we do, but how much love we put in the doing. It is not how much we give but how much love we put in the giving. "What we can take away from Mother

Teresa's quote is that love must be the core of every action of service we take, as she exemplified in her ministry.

She started by teaching the children of the slums, an endeavor she truly enjoyed. Though she had no proper equipment, she made use of what was available; writing in the dirt. She desired to make the children of the poor, literate, and to teach them how to care for themselves.

As they grew to know her, she gradually began visiting the poor and the sick, tending to them and their families, while others crowded around to watch in their squalid shacks. Eventually, she ministered and taught to greater and greater numbers.

Mother Teresa found a never-ending stream of human needs in the poor she met, often becoming exhausted and overwhelmed. Despite this weariness, she never forgot her prayer, finding it to be a source of support, strength, and blessing for all her ministry; "God does not expect us to do great things perfectly, just little things with great love."

In Mitch Albom's book *Tuesdays with Morrie,* Albom states, "The most important thing in life is to learn how to give out love, and how to let it come to us." This bestselling memoir chronicles the time Albom spent with his mentor, Morrie Schwartz, in the last few months of Schwartz's life. He transformed his death sentence into a final class, a lesson on how to live and how to love. According to Morrie, "Love is how you stay alive, even after you are gone." When you love others and allow yourself to be loved, that love lives on long after you are gone.

The love that Morrie showed Albom allowed him to reach out and rekindle that relationship, even as he lay dying. He deeply believed that love lasts forever; it cannot die. This was the lesson he wished to impart to those closest to him. What started as a modest labor of love to help cover some of Morrie Schwartz's medical bills, has now sold more than fourteen million copies in over fifty editions around the world; that is the power of love.

Practical Ways to Implement the Decision

There are many practical opportunities to implement your decision to love unconditionally. Explore some of these opportunities to develop and demonstrate your love for others, with specific and practical ways of showing your love. These are techniques that can be applied to every relationship in your life. Listed below are some techniques that you can use to increase caring, communication, and connection with others. They highlight how you can say "I love you" without using the actual words.

- *Focus on good communication with others.* Be kind and courteous when you have conversations. Ask questions about others' opinions, feelings, and thoughts. Be an active listener and a good sounding board. Most importantly, give people your undivided attention when communicating with them.

- *Fully embrace the present.* Choose to spend time with those you love. Show gratitude for them by lavishing them with praise. Take every opportunity to express your pride by complimenting them in front of others. With love, stay fully present in these moments. Focus on this conversation and not the one that took place yesterday or the one you may have tomorrow.

- *Take action; don't wait for others to reach out to you.* Show your love by making the first move. Leave notes or send letters and emails to show assurances of your love, attention, and affection. Reaching out can make you vulnerable, but it also brings you out from behind your walls. When we express our love for others, we will find ourselves the recipients of more love. Make a list of people you want to encourage, praise, or send a kind word to, and make it a goal to write them each a small note over the next six months.

- *Experiment with new ways of showing your love and accepting the gift of love from others.* You should try new methods of loving and accepting love to find out what works for you. Maybe talking or texting on the phone for a few minutes is a good way to connect, or perhaps joining someone on a quick walk around the block. Solving problems together is a great way to demonstrate the sharing and acceptance of love. From crossword puzzles to world peace, discussing solutions and finding answers together helps build open and loving communication.

- *Surround yourself with love. Be mindful that you love and that you are loved in return.* A small mirror with pictures along the sides, or a table filled with framed photos of loved ones can be a warm and wonderful reminder of all the love in your life.

- *Demonstrate and develop your love every day.* Deciding that love is the greatest gift of all is something you must develop daily. Love is like a muscle that needs to be flexed every day to stay supple and strong. Having discussions, sharing ideas, making new beginnings, or sharing fond memories are all examples of good exercises you can use to keep your 'muscles' in good shape. Love is about giving what nurtures another person. Soon, you will find that loving and giving are inseparable!

- ***Sometimes, we must agree to disagree.*** A great example of loving your neighbor is agreeing to disagree peacefully and respectfully when we see things differently, or we don't see eye to eye on a particular matter. It comes down to showing respect for, and even celebrating, one another's differences, but also emphasizing the matters that we do agree upon for the sake of unity. It shouldn't be expected that we will agree on everything. Diversity is a gift that allows us to build and strengthen unconditional love. We must learn how to respect and honor diversity because each of us is uniquely designed.

Takeaways

Loving relationships are a wonderful source of support, encouragement, and inspiration throughout our lives. The love that motivates us may be for self, family, mankind, or God. It is love that moves us to help others. It gives us the desire to leave something behind that continues to make the world a better place long after we are gone. Love can compel us to make changes, take risks, and take better care of ourselves.

Learning to love may not always be an automatic response, and many people struggle with receiving and expressing love. Maybe you were raised in a home that was heavy on discipline and short on praise or lacked deep expressions of affection. You might find it hard to accept simple gifts of love, such as kind words and tender gestures. Start slowly, and when you find yourself in these situations, stop and take a moment to change your focus. Instead of thinking of yourself and how you are reacting in this situation, think of what this gesture, this hug or small praise, means to the other person.

When you accept the hospitality that other people have to offer, you open yourself up to the life-changing ebb and flow of love. It's the love you have for yourself that makes you confident enough to try something new; something you might not otherwise pursue. It's the love of another person that compels you to be selfless enough to put yourself out there and to take risks. It is the love of God that assures you that it's perfectly all right to come up short because you know that God loves you unconditionally and eternally.

So, it's your decision. Make the choice to accept love as the greatest gift of all mankind, and never be afraid to love.

Chapter 2

Decide to Be Happy – Right Now

"Now when Jesus saw the crowds, he went up on a mountainside and sat down. His disciples came to him, and he began to teach them. He said..."

-Matthew 5:1-2

Opening Discussion

In the Introduction story, professor Alyssa said, "Happiness is not determined by your situation. Your state of happiness is determined by you." Being happy is a choice; one that we are solely responsible for. Some people seem naturally inclined to be happy, while for others, achieving happiness is a constant uphill battle.

Often, people long to be happy but don't have a clue how to achieve it. Many of us are conditioned from birth to be victims of our circumstances. As children, we learn this behavior from our parents or other adults around us, and it's not because they're purposely doing this; they're merely continuing the cycle from their own upbringing. It's difficult to break out of a negative environment, especially when we don't recognize it for what it is. We may not realize the times that we allow ourselves to be negatively impacted by our environment - or even our own negatively skewed inner-thoughts. This in turn, prevents us from feeling happy.

Take a game of golf, for example. On a par-3 hole where there is water in front of the green, one golfer might think to himself, "I hope I don't hit the ball into the water." His thoughts become so consumed with not hitting the ball into the water that when he finally hits the ball, it goes directly into the water.

His golfing buddy, on the other hand, pays no attention to the water at all. Her thoughts are completely focused on landing the ball gently on the green somewhere near the hole. Her odds of missing the water and landing on the green are much higher because she's focusing on the positive rather than the negative.

Likewise, if someone is always spending time around people who have a generally negative outlook on life, it can be difficult for them to avoid having the same perspective. Negativity and positivity are energies emitted by people, and because they tend to be highly contagious, it's incredibly important to surround ourselves with positive-minded people. Ensuring that our environment and thoughts are as positive as possible will aid us in our quest to happiness.

Jesus begins the Sermon on the Mount with a classic recipe for happiness, commonly called the "Beatitudes." The very first words of Jesus' ministry talk about Godly happiness, and how it can be obtained. In the

Gospel of Matthew 5:3-11, Jesus discusses the poor in spirit, the mourners, the meek; those who hunger and thirst for righteousness, those who are merciful and pure in heart; those who are peacemakers, and those who are persecuted for Christ's sake. All of these have assured rewards, both now, and in the coming kingdom.

The assurances can be found in the use of the word 'blessed.' The original Greek word for blessed is 'makarios,' which loosely translates to mean 'blissfully happy.' The blessing that Jesus is describing in his Sermon on the Mount is all-weather happiness that the storms of life cannot blow away. We need to hear this, now more than ever. Never before have people spent so much time and effort in trying to be happy, and yet, happiness has never seemed further from our grasp.

Historical Perspective

The word 'happy' originated in the late fourteenth century and was associated with being lucky, favored by fortune, and achieving prosperity. The word 'hap' related to events turning out well, in regards to chance or fortune. As the origins of the word imply, happiness became associated with happenings, happenstance, luck, and fortune. Therefore, it would seem that if circumstances are favorable, you are happy. If not, you are unhappy. Contrary to origins or popular belief, however, happiness is not a matter of chance or circumstance; it's a matter of choice.

"A happy life consists not in the absence, but in the mastery of hardships." This quote from Helen Keller is a testament to the person who chooses happiness despite overwhelming obstacles. Deaf and blind from the age of two, Helen knew first-hand what it was like to struggle with hardships, and yet, she was known for her unwavering optimism throughout her entire lifetime. Faced with seemingly impossible odds, she chose to optimistically put one foot in front of the other, every day. We can all take away a lesson from Helen Keller's example, and we too, can make the choice to change our lives for the better. If we choose to wake up every day and take another step forward toward greater happiness, there is no telling where it will lead us.

Many times, the source of our unhappiness is our own flawed perception of success and failure. We have this image in our minds that shows us that success and failure equal good and bad, respectively. This image is deceiving. In actuality, truly successful and happy people welcome failure, for they know that with every failure comes a lesson; an opportunity to learn, and grow, and get better. The failures also compel us to truly appreciate our eventual success and act as a reminder that nothing in the world worth having will be easy to come by.

Most of us have read or heard stories of famous people failing, often repeatedly, before finally finding success. Albert Einstein was considered mentally slow as a child, and now his name is synonymous with intelligence. Babe Ruth is one of baseball's all-time best home run hitters, yet he also held the highest strikeout record for decades, earning him the title 'King of Strikeout.' John Milton didn't let the loss of his eyesight stop him from writing *Paradise Lost*. Stephen Hawking went on to become one of the world's leading theoretical physicists after being diagnosed with amyotrophic lateral sclerosis (ALS), also called Lou Gehrig's disease in North America. Dr. Hawking's book, *A Brief History of Time*, became a bestseller, selling over 10 million copies. None of these people allowed failure or challenges to stop them from achieving their goals. When we come to understand that failure is merely a prelude to success, our state of happiness can be positively impacted.

The Decision in Action

"Your happiness grows in direct proportion to your acceptance and in inverse proportion to your expectations." -Michael J Fox

When actor Michael J. Fox was diagnosed with Parkinson's disease in 1991, he never imagined that such a diagnosis would redefine the way he looked at life, for the better. Rather than allowing himself to become defined by his limitations, Fox has learned to view life through different lenses. He realized that happiness is a choice, a new window through which to see life.

When we choose to expand the framework in which we view our circumstances, the more vivid the picture becomes. As a companion piece to his book, *Always Looking Up*, Fox filmed a documentary entitled *Adventures of an Incurable Optimist*. His goal in making the documentary was to determine why some people are constantly optimistic, despite the sometimes less-than-ideal circumstances they find themselves in. He also wanted to explore whether there was a direct connection between being hopeful and positive, and how that affects our happiness and quality of life. Fox himself is an excellent role model for seeing the glass as half full, by showing grace and an undying sense of humor, even in the face of the debilitating effects of Parkinson's.

The highlight of the documentary is when Fox makes a pilgrimage to Bhutan, a small Buddhist nation located between China and India. Instead of a Gross National Product, this tiny realm has a government policy that dictates happiness, with a national measure of Gross National Happiness. According to an article in the New York Times, the Bhutanese constitution clearly states that government programs will be judged by the happiness they create rather than by the money they generate. Bhutan's former Prime Minister, Jigme Thinley, describes happiness as "Complete well-being…being content with what is and with what one has." At one point during the segment, Fox discovers that being surrounded by such happiness has diminished the severity of his Parkinson's symptoms; he finds himself able to hike up a mountain without difficulty and notices that many of the physical challenges that plague him daily have dissipated. Overall, this natural optimist just felt better, proving something we all know intuitively – being surrounded by happiness is infectious and has a profound effect on our general dispositions and physical well-being.

There is a direct connection between focusing on positive energy, surrounding ourselves with optimism, and how it personally influences us. This is noteworthy because while many people believe that happiness is something that happens to them, the Bhutanese are quietly proving that happiness takes work and that we must make the conscious choice to share encouragement, smiles, and goodwill. Ultimately, that choice will not only have an effect on our lifestyle but will also affect those in our direct vicinity by association. Happiness takes work and planning; it doesn't depend on what you have, but on who you are and what you choose to focus on.

Practical Ways to Implement the Decision

"To get up each morning with the resolve to be happy...is to set our own conditions to the events of each day. To do this is to condition circumstances instead of being conditioned by them." This quote from Ralph Waldo Trine perfectly illustrates how happiness is not a matter of chance but a matter of choice. You truly can be as happy as you decide to be. Happiness is not controlled by an outside source, but rather by what is going on inside your own mind. Here are a few ways to help make happiness an easier choice to make, day by day:

- ***Don't hang out with the downer's club.*** These are people who get together to gossip and complain. If you associate with such individuals, then you will undoubtedly also become a "downer." Instead, surround yourself with positive, like-minded individuals; their positivity will undeniably rub off on you.

- ***Make it a habit to enjoy the moment.*** As strange as it may sound, the ability to appreciate what's right in front of you has very little to do with what you actually have. It's more about how you measure and assign value to the good things in your life at any given time. Simply practice wanting what you already have, and you'll find that you have what you want. Take a look around— what is in front of you that you can enjoy right now?

- ***Decide to smile more often than not.*** A smile conveys a visible sense of happiness, and various studies consider smiling to be highly contagious. When we smile, it sends a signal that others automatically respond to, making those around us feel better simply because they see us smile. Make a conscious effort to

35

Dr. Milton Mattox

share a smile with the next person you see; you may find that brightening someone else's day will also brighten your own.

- ***Accentuate the positive and minimize the negative.*** When life hands you lemons, think of all the different things you can do with those lemons. Of course, you could make lemonade! Concentrating on the negative aspects of life will only give them more importance and accentuate your negative emotions. The next time you find yourself facing an obstacle or a setback, reevaluate the situation in terms of what is good and focus on trying to make the best of it. You can usually find some positive in any negative situation, even if it's only a speck. Focus on that and move forward.

- ***Take time to notice and appreciate the details.*** Consistent, long term happiness depends on your ability to find joy in the small things. Even if you were to get everything you ever wanted, you would still be subject to the daily highs and lows that life has to offer. Think about the little things that bring you joy; the sound of rain on a tin roof, ocean waves crashing against a rocky shore as you doze off to sleep, spending time with your pets, or enjoying a beautiful sunset. When you focus on life's simple pleasures, you'll find you have an endless variety of things to appreciate, no matter the challenges in your life.

- ***Treat every day as a new opportunity to be better than yesterday.*** By setting mini-goals and focusing on small improvements, you'll find yourself naturally moving towards achieving bigger and better dreams. Your self-esteem and happiness will naturally increase along the way too. Celebrate the small victories and watch them turn into big ones!

- *Happiness grows in connection with others.* The Dalai Lama wrote, "We survive here in dependence on others. Whether we like it or not, there is hardly a moment of our lives when we do not benefit from others' activities. For this reason, it is hardly surprising that most of our happiness arises in the context of our relationships with others." Be generous with your compassion and your time, and listen when your friends have problems they need to talk about. A skillful listener can bring joy to everyone she encounters because we all need someone to talk to at one time or another. Others will notice your actions and you might motivate them to do the same.

- *Make a commitment to practice daily gratitude.* You've undoubtedly heard the saying "count your blessings" at some point in your life; it's actually sound advice. Practice daily gratitude by recalling all of the good things you've been blessed with. It might not always be easy, but try being thankful for the relationships with people in your life who matter to you. For example, be grateful for a loving and faithful husband or wife who works hard to provide for you and your family. Bring to mind all the people who enrich your life and who make a positive difference. Practicing daily gratitude will shift your mental focus off the things you don't have onto the blessings you do have. It will help you have a more grateful and humble attitude, as well as compassion, for those who are less fortunate.

- *Get rid of the negative self-talk in your mind.* Expel the negative thoughts from your mind like they are poison. You might have heard the saying, "you are what you think." This is because what you think determines what you feel, and what you feel determines your actions. It's true that we are our own worst critics. Critical self-talk, if left unchecked, can often lead to a perpetually negative attitude, and even a state of depression, low self-esteem, and severe lack of confidence. Learn to recognize negative self-talk when it happens, and make a conscious effort to reverse it by immediately replacing it with a positive affirmation. It might not feel natural at first, but as the English aphorism suggests, fake it until you make it, and in no time you'll have silenced your inner-bully.

Positive affirmations can be extremely powerful in transforming the way you think and feel about yourself. Repeat affirmations such as "I'm beautiful, I'm smart and intelligent and I'm always on time." For most of us this requires diligence and daily practice. Keep saying these positive affirmations until you start to positively change the way you view yourself. Make saying positive affirmations part of your daily routine.

Additionally, remove any and all negative news stories you hear on the radio and television. Most of what is reported on the news these days is negative and subjective talk instead of factual and objective. Over time, one can start feeling down and depressed. Instead, purposely and selectively choose the news stories that are objective, positive, and uplifting.

- *Live your passion.* Happiness embodies what you enjoy doing the most in your life. Nothing is more fulfilling and satisfying than doing what you love. Finding your sense of passion and purpose can sometimes be challenging, but it's not impossible.

Until you find your life's passion and purpose, you will live a life of mediocrity. Invest some quality time with yourself and do some soul-searching. What do you feel passionate about? What gives you purpose? Find those things and, if possible, make them your life's work. If that's not an option, then at least dedicate some time to it every day. Unlock your passion so you can enjoy an abundant life filled with joy and happiness.

It is important to note that what makes you happy is deeply personal. What makes you happy may be very different from what makes someone else happy. For example, some of my family members, friends, and colleagues constantly tell me that I work too much. They say that I should take more time to enjoy myself. What they don't realize is that I thoroughly enjoy what I do. To me, there is no labor in the work that I do. I do what I do because it makes me happy. Be careful to focus on what makes you happy and not someone else's definition of happiness.

Takeaways

The more we remember that life is a gift—that change is constant, and that we can't always be in control, the more we recognize and believe that happiness is a choice. Finding joy and happiness in the present moment, no matter how inadequate it may seem, makes a noticeable difference in your life and in the lives of those around you. While we all have different dreams and life goals, for most of us, living a meaningful life that positively influences others is important. Happiness isn't so much about what you have, because life evolves and your 'blessings' change.

What you can control, and use consistently, is your interpretation of your circumstances.

Contrary to what you may have heard, happiness is not a matter of chance, but a matter of choice. As Dale Carnegie said, "It isn't what you have, or who you are, or where you are, or what you are doing that makes you happy or unhappy. It is what you think about." When you choose to be happy, no one can take that away from you. Circumstance can't take it away because circumstance didn't create it. How will you choose to tune in to happiness right now? It's your decision. Decide, right now, to infuse a state of happiness into your life today.

Chapter 3

Decide That "It" Is Easy—Not Hard

Jesus replied, "Truly I tell you, if you have faith and do not doubt, not only can you do what was done to the fig tree, but also you can say to this mountain, 'Go, throw yourself into the sea,' and it will be done."

- Matthew 21:21

Opening Discussion

Jesus' lesson of faith, the moving of mountains, is a metaphor for accomplishing what seems impossible with relative ease. 'Mountain moving' doesn't require an inordinate amount of courage; it requires faith. The truth is, if you have faith, a belief that you can do something regardless of obstacles, you will accomplish virtually anything you set

41

your mind to. If you have faith that success is imminent, then it shall come to pass.

This is not a new concept by any means, it has been around since the dawn of time. Surprisingly, most people do not know about this concept; you can accomplish most things you set your mind to by possessing an unwavering belief that you've already succeeded. This concept has been given many names; most recently, the law of attraction. Additionally, Earl Nightingale discussed this notion back in 1950 during a recording he made called *The Strangest Secret*. According to Nightingale, the strangest secret is simply, "We become what we think about."

Similarly, Mark 9:23 states, "All things are possible for one who believes." Set your mind on what you want to achieve and believe without a doubt that you will succeed. Inevitably, there will be times when circumstances and situations cause us to waiver despite our best efforts. Here, it can be helpful to remind ourselves that without mountains, our faith would never be put to the test. Testing and refining, while rarely easy or enjoyable, are what make us grow and learn to tackle difficulties with ease, and even serenity. Circumstances and situations do not determine how successful you are; you, and you alone, make that determination.

Historical Perspective

The word 'easy' dates from the thirteenth-century, and is from the French 'aise,' which means 'comfortable,' or 'at ease.' The term became associated with 'not being difficult to deal with' in the mid-1400s, and 'comfortable' later in the fifteenth century. The history of the word 'difficult' has its roots in the Greek word 'kratos,' which means 'strength,' and 'kratys,' meaning 'strong.' The root of these Greek words is 'kar,' which means 'hard.' The use of the word 'difficult' in its current context began during the thirteenth century. Interestingly, the French word 'difficile' is a combination of 'dis'—'not, away from,' and 'facilis,' meaning 'easy.'

History contains many examples of seemingly impossible feats that were accomplished by sheer effort and human ingenuity. Above the hills of Cusco, Peru, you'll find the ruins of a colossal structure, with a rock wall longer than a football field. The wall, known as Saqsaywaman, took seventy-seven years to build, from 1431-1508. It is constructed of large stones, some of which are estimated to be over sixty tons, each intricately placed within the wall. Upon closer observation, it looks like the stones were cut with precision as if a laser or other modern tool was used. The stones are packed together so tightly that even a piece of paper cannot fit between them. Obviously, there were no lasers in the fifteenth century, only the arduous task of getting those enormous rocks in place. What is even more astounding is that these stones were quarried from the opposite side of the mound! How could an ancient civilization achieve this?

The ancient Egyptians built the great pyramids with similar obstacles and limitations. These accomplishments in human history were not only difficult, but given the environment and state of the world at the time, must have seemed impossible. Yet, someone believed that the pyramids could be built, just as someone believed the Great Wall of China could protect the ancient Chinese from the invading Mongols. Believing that it *was* possible, coupled with hard work and determination, helped to create each of these monumental wonders of the world which stand to this day; an epic testament to the power of belief.

The Decision in Action

On May 27, 1995, actor Christopher Reeve was paralyzed from a spinal cord injury. His injuries were so acute that he considered the reality that it might be better for his loved ones if he were to die. Not only did Reeve choose to live, but he also chose to use his celebrity status to advocate on behalf of the disabled. He is quoted as saying, "So many of our dreams at first seem impossible, then they seem improbable, and then, when we summon the will, they soon become inevitable." As a result of his courage, determination, and belief that he could make a difference despite his severe limitations, he made tremendous gains for the disabled community.

Through his leadership, Reeve and his wife Dana created the Christopher and Dana Reeve Foundation, an organization that has helped to educate the world about the need for more spinal repair research. Appearing before the United States Congress as a patient advocate, he increased funding and attention to the issue on a national level. Dana Reeve went on to establish the Quality of Life Grants Program, an organization that works to enhance the quality of life for those living with the daily challenges of a disability. Reeve knew that his fame could elevate awareness of spinal injuries to an international level. Despite his physical limitations, he spent the rest of his life reaching greater heights than he ever imagined.

Before 1903, no one believed that Wilbur and Orville Wright, or anyone for that matter, could build a machine that would fly through the air. Bicycle repairmen by trade, they had a vision and were unbending in their belief of it. Despite their limited experience with flight and the prevailing mindset that no machine heavier than air could soar through the sky, the brothers eventually succeeded; they have gone down in history books as the inventors of the first successful flying machines and revolutionized the way we travel. Their belief that flight was possible and that they could make it a reality, made all the difference. They decided that "it" could be done, and the results of their confidence and determination are in evidence today in every airport across the world.

Practical Ways to Implement the Decision

Nelson Mandela said, "It always seems impossible until it is done." When people say something is impossible, what they usually mean is, "I can't imagine how that could be possible, given the circumstances." For Mandela, it meant that life shouldn't be taken for granted, but rather, should be lived to the fullest with enthusiasm, inquisitiveness, and thankfulness. The message itself is powerful, but it is the messenger who gives it deep significance. Imprisoned for his political activism for twenty-seven years, Mandela went on to receive a Nobel Peace Prize and was inaugurated as the first black President of South Africa. Despite his circumstances, he believed that he could go on to accomplish great things; and he did, leaving behind a legacy that has inspired millions around the world.

We can choose to make a difficult task easier by shifting our thinking and putting into practice some of the following tips and techniques:

- *Decide to make something happen.* Take all the steps necessary to make things happen. There's a huge difference between knowing how to do something and actually doing it. Knowledge and intelligence are important, but taking action is the key ingredient to reaching our goals.

- ***Absorb yourself in the process of going after your dreams and goals.*** Once you have made the decision to move forward, take a deep breath and get down to business. Progress will come as you take action and move towards your goal. Make a plan for dealing with problems as they arise.

- ***Start small.*** The basic act of getting started and moving forward will supply you with all the motivation you need. Begin with just one activity or component of the larger goal, and you will find the momentum to continue to put one foot in front of the other. As Henry Ford said, "Nothing is particularly hard if you divide it into small pieces." For example, I'm often asked how to go about writing a book. My response is to ensure that each day you write one sentence, one paragraph, one page, or one chapter. Some days, the words flow and I can write a chapter with ease. Other days, the words are hard to come by so all I can muster is a single sentence. As long as I write something each day, even if it is only a sentence or two, I know that I will eventually finish the book because I started small as opposed to not starting at all.

- ***Remind yourself that the results are more important than the time it takes to achieve them.*** The walls of Saqsaywaman took more than seventy-seven years to build, and the construction of the Great Wall of China spanned a thousand years. La Sagrada Familia in Barcelona, Spain, has been under construction since 1882, and is now closer to completion than ever before. Each of these historic landmarks required generations of laborers to contribute to the building process. Understand that change won't happen overnight, and be diligent in continuing your consistent progress.

- *Concentrate on getting "it" done, not on getting "it" done perfectly.* While we may wish for perfection, 'good enough' is often the most productive path. The key to getting things done is to accept that more often than not, things won't be completed to our definition of perfection. So, take heart and learn from the mistakes you will inevitably make as you progress. Repeat this process repeatedly until you've reached your goal. The most significant impediment to achieving your goals is the elusive quest for perfection. Always remember that perfection is subjective, and it's not the outcome of the task; it is the achievement of completing the task that matters the most.

- *Concentrate on your enthusiasm to get "it" done.* Focus on the excitement that reaching your goals will bring you. Ignore the overwhelming aspects of what it will take to get 'it' done, and focus on the end goal. Charles Buxton said, "Success is due less to ability than to zeal." This philosophy holds true for achieving any of your goals.

Takeaways

So many of us live our lives in a daze, content to simply get by rather than reach for our dreams because we deem them to be impossible or too fantastical. Real growth occurs when what you know changes how you act and how you choose to live. Have faith in your abilities and the strength of your convictions to reach your objective and get 'it' done. When you choose to follow your vision, you will find yourself approaching your activities with confidence and a new sense of purpose.

The decision you've made to view 'it' as possible, will ease the setbacks and failures you'll encounter along the way. These obstacles are temporary conditions that you can work through when you focus on your goals and dreams. You may get knocked down, but with the right positive perspective, you'll get back up and take your next step. History has proven time and again that amazing results are born from those who set goals that were previously thought to be unrealistic or impossible. The things deemed unattainable and beyond reach are yours for the taking when you decide that 'it' is easy, not hard.

Chapter 4

Decide to Hug Someone Today—You'll Make Their Day

"And he took the children in his arms, placed his hands on them and blessed them. "

-Mark 10:16

Opening Discussion

Jesus knew the importance of physical touch in communicating with people, in expressing encouragement, affirmation, and in bringing healing. In this verse, we see not only the power that comes from an embrace, but also the value of accepting the simple act of human touch. Children are often in a place where all they can do is receive. They don't allow self-sufficient pride, or being uncomfortable with physical intimacy, to get in the way of accepting the gift of human touch. Someone in your life needs to feel the tenderness of a warm embrace. Could that someone be you?

Historical Perspective

The first known appearance of the word 'hug' is believed to be during the 1560s, and possibly originated from Scandinavia, and the Norweigian word 'hugga,' which meant, 'to soothe.' Another variant is the Old English 'hycgan,' which is 'to think or consider.' There is an interesting similarity between these ancient words and the German word 'hegen,' which translates to, 'to foster, cherish' and was developed from the earlier meaning, 'to enclose with a hedge.' Hugs themselves seem to be a truly universal show of affection. They form a language that requires no words but is understood by all. Different cultures, however, are more open to hugging than others. The Japanese, for example, prefer bowing to hugging, while many Middle Eastern, Mediterranean and South American cultures typically embrace one another with enthusiastic bear hugs. These cultures are considered "high touch" cultures, while North America, Northern Europe and Australian are considered more "low touch." The unspoken connection that people feel after sharing a hug indicates that hugs actually hold the power to strengthen our social relationships.

When we hug someone, whether it be a full-body hug, an abbreviated side hug, or even laying a hand on their shoulder, we are communicating an intimacy that may not be appreciated or welcome. It's crucial, especially in this day and age, to keep in mind the cultural differences, as well as gender and generational distinctions. Be mindful that various cultures have different boundaries and expectations. It's also important not to forget that some people just don't like to be touched; it's a good idea to first ask someone if you can hug them, especially if you don't know them intimately.

The Decision in Action

As human beings, we are unique and extraordinarily complex. There are many ingredients that go into creating a happy, healthy, fully functioning person. Jack Canfield, a motivational speaker and co-creator of the *Chicken Soup for the Soul* book series, explains that hugs and human touch are key aspects of helping us feel complete and whole. In the story titled, 'The Hugging Judge,' Canfield tells the story of Lee Shapiro, a retired judge who understood the importance of sharing a hug. He began by offering everyone a little red heart in exchange for a hug, and soon became a minor celebrity, known for spreading his message of love. He accepted the challenge of hugging anyone and everyone. Perhaps his biggest test came when he visited a home for the terminally ill, severely mentally handicapped, and quadriplegic. As the story goes, Shapiro, accompanied by a team of doctors and nurses, went about this routine of hugging people and handing out little red hearts. The last person he came to was a man named Leonard, whom Shapiro saw was drooling onto his big white bib. Although he doubted he could ever get through to this man, he nonetheless reached over and gave Leonard a hug. This is what followed, in the author's words:

"All of a sudden, Leonard began to squeal: "Eeeeehh! Eeeeehh!" Some of the other patients in the room began to clang things together. Shapiro turned

to the staff for some sort of explanation, only to find that every doctor, nurse and orderly was crying. Shapiro asked the head nurse: "What's going on?" Shapiro will never forget what she said: "This is the first time in 23 years we've ever seen Leonard smile."

Sometimes, it only takes a hug; a small, heartfelt embrace, to change our lives and the lives of others, forever.

Hugging is unique in that it is typically a joint experience; it is rather rare to hug someone without getting a hug in return. In his book, *Beyond Reason*, Gregg Korbon describes the different ways in which people interacted with him during and after the sudden death of his nine-year-old son, Brian. He became aware of his internal reactions when he received a handshake, a hand on the shoulder, and a hug. He took note of the variety of hugs he received from friends, family, and co-workers, and observed that the most immediately satisfying hug is the 'belly hug.' He describes the belly hug as one in which you embrace each other with both arms and create contact with your bellies and your heart, holding on tight. The feeling it produces is one of deep and profound connection. Korbon writes that the effects of belly hugs are so distinct that people can feel the difference instantly. Belly hugs loosen you up and break down the walls you tend to unknowingly build up throughout our day.

To observe the uncensored effects of hugs in action, look no further than the children in your life. Perhaps they are your children, grandchildren, nieces or nephews. Kids often instinctively know how to express great tenderness and receive affection in return. They crawl into your lap to hear a story read to them. They grip your hand as you walk down the sidewalk; they clasp their little arms around your neck in a tender embrace. They are not shy about giving hugs or asking for them.

However, as we grow up, we become more reserved when it comes to asking for hugs, or showing physical affection in general. We start hearing and listening to lies such as, "You're a big boy now. You don't need to have a hug." I say 'lies' because there is no such thing as being too big, or too old, to need hugs. Yet we listen to, and believe, these words, and we stop touching, hugging, and holding each other. Human touch is a genuine physical need and if you want to get in tune with yourself, you should start reaching out and touching more people in your life. I promise, you'll feel better as a result. Hugs are thought to be so important and beneficial that there is a day set aside to celebrate the gift of a hug. In 1986, Kevin Zaborney - also sometimes referred to as the Ambassador of Hugs - declared January 21 as "National Hugging Day." According to the organizer's website, nationalhuggingday.com, the day was "created for family and friends to hug often and freely with one another."

Practical Ways to Implement the Decision

A hug can be a profound expression of affection, wrapped up in a simple gesture. They can further improve an already great situation, or help someone who's overcome with sadness to feel better. Not only do hugs help boost our moods and emotional dispositions, but studies suggest that they actually have the ability to improve one's physical health as well; researchers at the University of North Carolina at Chapel Hill found that a humble hug could lower blood pressure and reduce the harmful effects of stress.

- *A hug is a natural mood enhancer.* Dorothy M. Neddermeyer, PhD, is quoted as saying, "Hugging is all natural; it is organic, naturally sweet, no pesticides, non-fattening, no carbohydrates,

53

no preservative, no artificial or genetically engineered ingredients, and 100% wholesome."

- ***Touch the important people in your life on a regular basis.*** Starting today, give regular hugs to your children and spouse. If you're not a naturally affectionate person, it may seem unnatural at first, but you will learn to appreciate and welcome those connections. Human contact is as necessary to our overall health as vitamins and minerals are to our diet.

- ***Make sure your hugs are open, genuine, and freely given to others.*** In order for everyone to benefit from hugs, they need to be open and sincere. Some people don't like to be touched, so before you initiate a hug—whether it be with a complete stranger or someone you know who values their personal space—be sure to ask their permission. If they decline the offer, respect their decision and simply smile and offer sincere words of kindness instead. Many of us know at least one friend who adopted the "air hug" as a means of participating in the action of a hug without having to succumb to an actual physical embrace!

- ***We all benefit from hugs, no matter our age.*** Virginia Satir, a leading family therapist, suggests that everyone needs at least four hugs a day for healthy survival, eight hugs a day for emotional strength, and twelve hugs a day to grow and be empowered. If that sounds like too much hugging to you, start small; Start by giving your spouse or someone special in your life a hug at least once a day. Don't forget your children (the big ones and the little ones), or your friends and neighbors. As you go about your day, think about someone who might feel better if they received a hug.

- ***There is energy and power in hugging.*** Offering a hug to someone who needs one makes us more conscious of those around us and allows us to share the power of kindness and goodness. But that feeling you get - that surge of energy - is actually a positive, hormonal boost of oxytocin. This is what's responsible for that jolt of 'feel good' you get when you hug someone, and they hug you back.

- ***Personal touch is not just about intention; it's also about perception.*** Remember that intimacy may not come naturally to everyone, including yourself. Many of us have to work towards a goal of giving and receiving touch, no matter how passive or slight the contact. Rather than keeping love at an arm's length, be encouraged to reach out and hug someone.

Takeaways

Henri Jozef Machiel Nouwen was a Dutch-born Catholic priest and writer who authored forty books about spirituality. He speaks of an encounter he had with a young girl who asked for a blessing during one of his workshops. Nouwen writes how he went through the motions, giving her a sign of the cross and a quick blessing. The girl quickly responded, "No, I want a real blessing." He wrapped her in his priestly robe and hugged her tight; all the while telling her how wonderful she was, how important she is to God and to himself. After the hug, the girl looked up at Nouwen and he observed her spiritual radiance and renewed strength. Hugging, at its core, is a good medicine. It transfers energy from one person to another and, as the story suggests, gives the person who is being hugged an emotional lift. It conveys a special kind of unspoken communication between two people, when you don't have the words. The best part of a hug is that you usually can't give one without getting one. With permission, decide to hug someone today—you'll make their day, and yours.

Chapter 5

Decide to Genuinely Listen to People More Often Than You Speak

"Whoever has ears, let them hear."

- Matthew 11:15

Opening Discussion

It's very easy to slip into what the Bible calls 'dullness of hearing'; to hear without faith and to see little or no moral fruit in our lives as a result. As Jesus makes clear in this scripture, ultimately, it's how we hear that reveals who we truly are. Not everyone has spiritual ears or the ability to understand things of a higher nature. But for those who do understand, they should consider the importance of these words and attend to the needs of others. The notion of 'hearing' isn't just limited to Christianity, this Scripture from Matthew is also found in Jewish writings, "He that hears let him hear, and he that understandeth let him understand." These writings illustrate that God requires us to use the gifts He has given us, and to improve on them if we can. If you have ears, listen. If you understand, then act.

Historical Perspective

In ancient civilizations, the skill of listening was necessary for communication, obtaining information, and passing on traditions. The word 'listen' can be found in many different languages. From the Old English word 'hlysnan,' 'to listen,' to the German 'lauschen,' also with the same meaning. The Greek word 'kleos,' meaning 'to report, rumor' or 'immortal glory' is also a part of the word listen's etymology. The Latin word 'cluere' means, 'to hear oneself called, to be spoken of.' The ancient Greek sage and philosopher Epictetus said, "We have two ears and one mouth so we can listen twice as much as we speak." Amazingly, he spoke those words almost 1400 years ago and yet, they continue to have such relevance to our lives today! His statement highlights the importance of listening; far more benefit is gained by listening twice as much as we speak. Epictetus states that we *can* listen instead of we "must" or we "should." His choice of words implies that listening is a choice, one that takes effort and is not automatic.

Reminding ourselves that we have two ears and one mouth is a useful approach to effective communication. If we listen more than we speak, we foster the same ability in others, acting as a model for positive and successful communication. If we listen closely, people will tell us everything we need to know. Not just with their words but also with their requests, recommendations, and even in the words they don't say, such as body language. Really listening is one of the keys to a deep and genuine understanding between one another.

The Decision in Action

Stephen Richards Covey was the author of the best-selling book *The Seven Habits of Highly Effective People*. A frequently discussed section of the book is "Habit 5: Seek first to understand, then to be understood." Covey understood the importance of opening yourself up to the person who is speaking, to the point of empathetic listening; feeling what they are feeling. He believed that the only way to establish communication in some professional and personal situations was by becoming the person you are listening to, even if just for a moment. Covey noted that it takes time to learn to listen empathically, and much practice to become adept at it. But when you do, you'll quickly realize that the rewards are invaluable. You'll achieve a whole new level of communication and problem solving because you'll see a situation from multiple points of view.

In his book, Covey recommends that the first person you listen to is yourself, to discover your true core values and goals. Once you define what's truly important, move on to the next phase; listening to others. When you tune in to what other people are saying, you become more aware of their values and goals. This helps you to find common ground, which in turn will allow you to maintain and develop productive relationships.

During the height of World War II, Winston Churchill positioned himself as a receiver; a great listener. He listened and engaged in conversations with people throughout the government, the military, and citizens around the world. His conversations were a means to gather more information and develop clarity, to help arrive at decisions that would ensure an allied victory over Nazi Germany. Churchill's famous quote, "Courage is what it takes to stand up and speak; courage is also what it takes to sit down and listen," illustrates how deeply he understood the power of listening in order to get an understanding of the bigger picture. In meetings, he would urge everyone to share their thoughts in an effort to get as many views as possible. In personal settings, he would listen with intense interest, often with playful quips and asides to indicate his interest. Active listening was one of Winston Churchill's greatest tools and he used it to gather information, motivate others, and communicate effectively. Indeed, his ability to listen undoubtedly fostered his skills as an empathetic speaker. His wartime broadcasts often consisted of words that he knew people *needed* to hear, rather than what he felt they *wanted* to hear.

Practical Ways to Implement the Decision

Listening is such a crucial activity, yet surprisingly, we devote so little effort to doing it well. Listening is essential for building healthy relationships and successful partnerships. Here are some essential tips and techniques that can help you to become a great listener and improve your interpersonal skills:

- *Focus on being present.* Show the person you are listening to that they have your undivided attention. Proper body language is key to demonstrating that you are listening actively. Sit up straight or lean forward slightly. Maintain eye contact and face the speaker.

- ***Focus on what the speaker is saying.*** Try not to think about what you are going to say next, instead, allow the speaker to finish their train of thought naturally. Be quiet and don't interrupt the other person or try to finish their sentences for them. Unless they specifically ask for your advice, assume they just want to talk it out. Let silence be your guide.

- ***Keep an open mind while you listen.*** Be sure to suspend judgment while you are listening, especially in your posture and facial expressions. Be aware of your non-verbal behavior to avoid appearing aggressive or defensive, and look for ways to encourage the speaker, like smiling or nodding. When you genuinely listen to people, you care about what they are saying. Show you care by tabling your opinion and asking open-ended questions about their opinions, beliefs, and needs.

- ***Minimize distractions while you have a conversation.*** Get rid of external distractions by turning off the television, putting your phone in your pocket, tuning out other conversations around you, or putting down your book or magazine. If your thoughts are keeping you from giving the speaker your full attention, let them go and redirect your focus solely on the person talking. Great listening is an extension of the Golden Rule; listen to others in the same manner as you would want them to listen to you.

- ***Respond appropriately to what the speaker is saying.*** To demonstrate that you're actively engaged in the conversation, use phrases like, "Really?" or, "Then what happened?" To show that you understand what is being said, you can use prompts like "I see" or, "Right." If you don't understand something, wait for a natural break to ask clarifying questions.

- **Be humble.** Great listening is hard work and requires a genuine desire to learn and understand others better. When you think about it, listening is actually civility at its highest level. Active listening is focusing on the other person and not yourself. When you are actively engaged in listening to someone else, you're less concerned with winning the argument or dominating the conversation. Instead, you are more concerned with gaining valuable insight and understanding.

As you practice your listening skills, learn to settle into silence and use it to better comprehend all points of view. While these ideas are good common sense, it does take regular practice and strong determination to develop good listening skills.

Takeaways

Effective listening skills fuel our social, emotional, and professional lives. Unlike other skills, however, listening is one that may not come naturally to some and requires a degree of practice and change in behavior. At its core, listening actively makes our loved ones feel more worthy, appreciated, and interesting. In our business relationships, taking the time to genuinely listen to others saves time and money by preventing misunderstandings and clarifying goals.

Strong communication brings about greater intimacy. When parents take the time to truly listen to their children, it helps to build their self-esteem. Everyday conversations take on new significance, and relationships deepen. When we decide to listen more than we speak, we foster the same skills in others by acting as a model for positive and effective communication. Most importantly, we gain a deeper understanding when we learn to just be quiet and listen. Decide today that you will listen at least twice as much as you speak.

Chapter 6

Decide to Be Healthy, Starting Right Now

"On hearing this, Jesus said it is not the healthy that need a doctor, but the sick.

-Matthew 9:12

Opening Discussion

These words from Jesus are an illustration of how important it is to make it our aim in life to be as healthy as we can. Good health ultimately affects all areas of our lives positively, from being more productive at work, at home, and in our community. When we have taken the stance that good health is a natural choice, we don't have to worry as much about poor health or illness, and can focus our energies elsewhere. To put it in the simplest terms—when we feel good, we can do good. We should strive to be in good physical shape so that we have more energy to help those who are less fortunate than we are.

Historical Perspective

The word 'healthy' was first found in the Proto-Germanic root word 'khailaz,' which translates exactly to, "to make whole." The Old English word 'haelp' also means, "wholeness, a being whole," but could also be used in the sense of "to make sound or well." This ultimately led to the English verb 'haelan,' which is, "to heal." The word 'health' has a similar history, by adding an abstract suffix, which denotes, "the condition of being well and sound." At that point, using the term healthy to mean, "possessing good health" was a quick jump. Healthy, health, and heal, all come from the same source and are as closely related as they appear to be.

Science is slowly beginning to confirm what some wise men have noted throughout history. It was King David who said, in Proverbs 17:22, "A cheerful heart is good medicine, but a crushed spirit dries up the bones." When you hear the word 'health,' you shouldn't think only of your physical health. The state of your mental health affects your physical health, which in turn affects your spiritual state of mind and overall quality of life. Just as the various words for 'healthy' are intertwined throughout history, the mind, body, and spirit, are similarly tied together.

Dr. Robert Muller, a peace activist and former Assistant Secretary-General of the United Nations, had much to say about being healthy, positive, and peaceful. Here's an excerpt from his one of his poems titled, "Decide to be healthy" which underscores the power of this decision:

"Decide to be healthy. Pray to God every day for good health. Take health as your sacred, God given duty. Make no room whatsoever for the slightest thought of sickness. Encourage your trillions of faithful little cells through joy, happiness and confidence."

Dr. Muller had many similar poems including, but not limited to, "Decide to be happy," "Decide to be peaceful," "Decide to be thankful," and "Decide to forgive." He was a firm believer that the decision to change our lives is clearly up to each of us. However, when it comes to being healthy, some think that good health is by happenstance and not the result of the decisions we make.

Unfortunately, many of us do not realize that we are truly a product of what we eat and whether or not we live an overly sedentary lifestyle. For example, the bodies of people who have Type 2 diabetes typically do not produce enough insulin to meet their needs. In some cases, the onset of Type 2 diabetes occurs when the body starts to become insulin resistant which means that the body's cells no longer respond normally to insulin. The body produces insulin to regulate the level of glucose in the blood, which is generally linked to how much sugar and carbohydrates we eat. When the body becomes insulin resistant, it needs more and more insulin to function normally. In some cases, eating food and drinks with too much sugar and certain types of carbohydrates causes the body to become insulin resistant, leading to Type 2 diabetes. This is just one example of what can cause Type 2 diabetes, there are other causes such as heredity. However, by working with qualified medical doctors and nutritionists, some individuals may thwart the onset of Type 2 diabetes by gradually lowering their daily intake of foods high in carbohydrates. Of course, this would be done under the strict guidance of qualified medical professionals. The main point here is that some people with Type 2 diabetes can help themselves tremendously by making a choice about the types of foods they eat.

The key to good health can begin from within, once you transform your mind, you can begin to transform your body. First, decide to be healthy, then let that decision guide you in making better choices in your health.

The Decision in Action

Deepak Chopra is an Indian-born American physician, public speaker, and writer. Chopra began his career as an endocrinologist, before later turning his focus to alternative medicine. He now runs his own medical center which places an emphasis on the connection between the mind and body. His focus has been to get people to take charge of their own wellness. Chopra concedes that this is a daunting challenge, as the pattern of making bad habits and poor lifestyle choices can be tough to break. The key, he says, is that the power to break our conditioning belongs to the same person who created it; the power lies with us. The turnaround is dependent on our commitment to replacing old behaviors and adopting new patterns. Once our mind begins to pay attention, it can adapt and change more easily. The general term Chopra uses is 'neuroplasticity,' which refers to our ability to apply awareness to discipline, mindfulness, and good intentions. In effect, the knowledge and power to create change in our bodies are already stored in our minds. It's sort of like we're preprogrammed, if you will. "The practical dilemma," states Chopra, "is how to use our strengths and motivation to help us remain committed to wellness as a lifetime pattern." We have the ability, if we tap into it, to apply positive thinking to being healthy.

"The thoughts we choose to think are the tools we use to paint the canvas of our lives," says Louise Hay. An American motivational author and metaphysical lecturer, Hay's international bestseller, *You Can Heal Your Life*, has sold more than fifty million copies worldwide. She believes that we are responsible for our own good health, or lack of it. From the foods we consume to the physical activity we participate in, and most importantly, to our thoughts—all of these contribute to our state of overall health. For more than thirty years, she has helped people discover the full potential of their own minds, and to propel personal growth as well as self-healing. Hay writes, "If our thoughts are fearful, angry, or in any way negative, then the chemicals that these messengers deposit *depress* our immune systems. If our thoughts are loving, optimistic, and positive, then the different chemicals that these messengers—or neuropeptides— deposit will *enhance* our immune system." She believes that moment-by-moment, we can choose healthy thoughts or unhealthy thoughts; the results are manifested in the state of our health. In this way, all of our thoughts are in charge of creating our future.

Practical Ways to Implement the Decision

More and more people in today's society are burdened with a multitude of health issues. We all know that we could, and should, do better when it comes to looking after our health. The motivations may vary from wanting to be healthy for our spouses or children, or a desire to keep up with, or take up an active lifestyle. Whatever the motivator, the outcome is the same—we begin to see that our physical health directly impacts the majority of our life experiences, as well as what we have to offer of ourselves to others and to the world.

By making a conscious choice to stay or to become healthy, it becomes more than a goal, it becomes a way of life. A goal is often focused on a fixed point, somewhere in the future. It typically has a deadline, so while it takes a lot of hard work and dedication to reach a goal, once achieved, it is over. A decision, on the other hand, is a resolve that permeates and dictates every moment, starting right here and now. Let's look at some of the steps you can take that will put you on the path to being the healthiest version of yourself:

- *Take time before starting and ending your day to give yourself a little pep talk.* As you wake up in the morning, think of the good experiences you are going to have and how great you are going to feel as you move about your day. At night, slow your thoughts down as you drift off to sleep. Review your day; concentrate on the things you learned, the opportunities you had, and the good health you experienced.

- *Find your motivation and inspiration.* Most people have a reason that they decide to be healthy. Many call it their 'Why.' Having a motivator, something deep down inside, can give you the power and resolve you need to keep going, even when the going gets tough. Let it help drive you and push you to complete your next workout, or to keep making healthy meal choices.

- ***Take time out each day to be still.*** We're all busy, but it's important to take time for ourselves. Make sure to carve out time during your day to sit in a quiet spot and reflect. Make it a priority to pray, meditate, or simply enjoy some solitude every day. It works out well if you can make it part of your daily routine, but sometimes just taking advantage of a quiet moment to decompress can make a big difference in your energy levels—physically, emotionally, and mentally.

- ***Your mother was right: getting enough sleep!*** When your body is not getting enough sleep, you may find yourself in an endless cycle of exhaustion. Aim for seven to eight hours of sleep every night and you will see a dramatic improvement in your energy levels.

- ***Get up and move your body everyday.*** There are small changes you can make that will have a big impact in the long run. Park in the farthest spot away from the entrance to the store, take an extra loop around the block while you walk the dog, or take the stairs instead of the elevator. Adding in more movement will increase your stamina and enhance your mood. It doesn't have to be an hour-long workout if you don't have that kind of time; just start by getting your body moving, and soon you will find you can, and want, to do more and more.

- ***Make it fun! Being healthy doesn't have to be a chore.*** If you don't enjoy running, try walking. Play tag with the kids, or have a dance party in the living room while you do the dusting. There are so many different ways to incorporate physical activities into your daily routine, it's important to find something you enjoy so that you won't return to your old bad habits.

71

Takeaways

When we ask ourselves what is important in life, many of us might answer that we want to make the most of each day that we are given here on Earth. Deciding to be healthy is a step in the right direction. Does that mean that every choice we make, every single day has to be perfectly healthy? Of course not! But when you make the decision to lead a healthy life, you make yourself and your health a priority. With a combination of powerful positive thinking and shifting of choices, there are no excuses that will deter you from staying the course, and keeping true to your goals. Wellness and vitality await you once you make the choice to be healthy, starting right now.

Chapter 7

Decide to Be the Person You Want to Be, and Be That Person—Starting Right Now

"Very truly I tell you," Jesus answered,
"before Abraham was born, I am!"

- John 8:58

Opening Discussion

In this powerful verse from Scripture, Jesus is revealed as the great 'I am.' The ancient Greek phrase is 'ego emi,' the same expression found in the Greek translation of the Old Testament, is used to describe the voice from the burning bush. By using the phrase 'I am,' Jesus is clearly and emphatically stating that he is Yahweh alone, the God of Israel. Jesus and his listeners would have been familiar with this phrase and known what it signified. Jesus knew who he was and boldly stated it.

The relevance and implications of this certainty are significant for your life, impacting all of mankind for eternity. Imagine the power you'd have if you decide to be the person you want to be and be that person starting right now.

Historical Perspective

When you are struggling with a decision about how to make changes in your life, there are certain motions you'll likely go through. You might create a lengthy list of pros and cons, seek wise counsel from friends, or pray and search for spiritual insight. In the end, despite all of the input and well-meaning intentions, it's up to you to make a choice. At the critical moment of decision, you may be willing to put your decision into action.

It's easy to become so wrapped up in the hustle and bustle of the daily grind that you never take the time to consider your path in life. Many of us are guilty of spending far too much of our time and energy on endeavors that really don't matter and keep us from focusing on what is most important. Our thoughts are often dominated by money, recognition, or celebrity, and cultural status. We may find ourselves wondering how we can achieve our true dreams; the ones that faded away during the business of life. So why not take control of who you are and become the person you want to be? That decision rests with you.

The Decision in Action

"It's not what's happening to you now or what has happened in your past that determines who you become. Rather, it's your decisions about what to focus on, what things mean to you, and what you're going to do about them that will determine your ultimate destiny." This quote from Tony Robbins sums up the power behind making decisions and following through on them. The truth is, changing who you are comes down to a simple concept, decide who you want to become and be that person.

Tony Robbins is the perfect example of someone who decided who he wanted to be and took steps to change his life accordingly. A motivational speaker who makes a living inspiring others to find the power within, Robbins is a bestselling self-help author and advisor to many leaders in sports, business, and government. He became determined to change his life after a particularly low period in which he was struggling to pay his bills, was unhealthy, overweight, and without direction. He not only transformed his own life, but he developed systems that would help change the lives of thousands of others.

Robbins says, "I personally believe that in order to get to where you want to be in life, no matter how successful or happy or fulfilled you are at this point, you have to be willing to understand that the same level of thinking that got you to where you are, is not going to get you to where you want to be." Once you decide who you want to be, you must move forward into that decision, and be *that* person. As Robbins points out, life is constantly evolving, and the repetitive thinking or action that got you where you are right now, must evolve and grow to get you to the next level; whatever the next level may look like for you.

Tyler Perry, now a household name known for his movies and plays, wasn't always a writer, producer, and director. It was thanks to a singular piece of advice that he heard while watching *The Oprah*

Winfrey Show that he changed his life forever. The episode discussed the therapeutic powers of writing down your thoughts, and this advice strongly resonated with Perry. Encouraged to write down his thoughts and experiences, he realized that he had stories he wanted to share, and ideas he wanted to impart to others. He began writing a series of letters to himself, in the voice of different characters. These letters eventually became the basis of the musical *I Know I've Been Changed*. Perry weathered several cycles of working, saving money, and putting on his play before he eventually found success. After hearing the advice on *The Oprah Winfrey Show* pertaining to the benefits of writing, Tyler Perry was able to release the creative genius that was deep inside of him, which led him to eventually become the person he had always envisioned.

He advises those who are seeking to find who they truly are and how to put those visions into action. His guidance is three-fold. Begin with following that 'gut-feeling' deep inside you that you're not being truthful to who you really are; you know, that nagging feeling that won't go away. Instead of being stuck in a 'prefabricated life,' a life that you believe others or society deems to be the correct path to follow, decide who *you* want to be. Second, plant the seed of who you want to be, watering it with the belief of your vision. Yes, other factors may contribute to its growth, but you must believe in the decision to change for it to take root. Finally, invest all of your energy into that decision and run with it! Perry says that we all get tossed in different directions by following every shifting idea that comes into our head. What separates the doers from the dreamers is that the doers take that one idea and stay with it until it becomes a reality.

Practical Ways to Implement the Decision

It's a challenge to find out who you are before you decide what you'll do. Many of us find out who we want to be through a process of elimination by discovering who we don't want to be! It is never too late to decide who you want to be or to put it into action. Here are some tips on how to deliver on your passion and purpose, starting right now.

- *Write down who you want to be.* There is something concrete about writing your ideas down on paper. Be sure to write it in the present tense so that you know that your goal is happening right now, rather than something that might occur in the future. Put it somewhere prominent, where you will see it every day. Your current goals should be in the form of what I call, 'I am', present tense statements, rather than 'I will be', future tense statements. For example, some of your goals could be, 'I am a writer,' 'I am a successful businesswoman,' and 'I am happy, healthy and benevolent.' By thinking and writing your goals in the present tense, the goals are already completed in your subconscious mind. In my experience, when this occurs, the universe will coalesce your goals into a series of events to help bring them to fruition.

- *Become the person you want to be by acting like that person.* With every deliberate action you take modeled after the image in your mind's eye, you move closer to being that person. Before too long, you'll look around and realize that you have become that person.

- *Be comfortable in your own skin! Remember that you are unique, there's no one else on earth like you!* Learn to embrace

77

and accept all that you are in order to become all that you can be. Your distinctive views, experiences, and originality are what set you apart from the rest. Bring your unique "brand" to everything you do.

- *Accept that you will make mistakes along the way, but there is value in the lessons your mistakes teach you.* Mistakes are more than just a part of life; they are a measure of your progress. Indeed, mistakes and failures are necessary steps toward eventual success. You typically learn more from your largest mistakes than from significant successes. If you don't fail from time to time, you're not stretching yourself and learning. Appreciate that you're constantly evolving and improving as you push yourself into becoming the person you want to be. Sometimes our greatest victories are born from our mistakes!

- *Give yourself affirmations that are related to what you want to do.* Affirmations should focus on "I am" and "I have" rather than "I want." Again, they should be worded in a way to reinforce the belief that you already have what you want. One of the best things about affirmations is their accessibility; you can use them anytime, anywhere you want. In addition to affirmations, visualizations are also helpful because seeing is believing. Instead of repeating a phrase, picture a new reality in your mind. Replay that vision whenever you need a boost.

- *Focus on the positive!* When you decide who you want to be and go for it, be sure to focus on the things you can control and let go of the rest. There are so many variables in life that are out of our control. By choosing to remain focused on the positive aspects of your decision, you can help keep frustration and disappointment under control by keeping things in perspective. Deciding to be who you want to be is a process; take it one step at a time.

Takeaways

"The tragedy of life is not that it ends so soon, but that we wait so long to begin it." -W.M. Lewis

So many dreams go unfulfilled, and far too many aspirations remain unexplored. From this moment on, start believing that you're ready for the next phase of your life to begin. Embrace what lies ahead knowing that the challenges, obstacles, and unknown which lie ahead are all part of the wonderful journey of becoming who you want to be. No matter your age, it is never too early or late to be who you want to be. At the age of 65, Harland David Sanders, best known as Colonel Sanders, started the now very successful Kentucky Fried Chicken. He did not let his age deter him from doing something that he always wanted to do. Decide to be who you want to be and be that person, starting right now!

Chapter 8

Putting Your Decision Into Practice

When you make a decision but fail to take action, it's as if you made no decision at all. In other words, decisions are powerless unless you make the effort to follow through with them. When you follow a decision cycle with action, there's a much better chance that the decision you made will end in success. Interestingly, the etymological meaning of 'succeed' is 'that which follows,' for success is difficult, and often impossible, without action. During the late fourteenth century, the word 'succeed' came into popularity, with the meaning, 'come next after, to take the place of another.' This term was coined from the Old French 'succeder' and Latin 'sucedere,' meaning, 'come after, go near to.' During the early fifteenth century, the meaning changed slightly, to 'to continue, endure' and the first record of 'succeed' being used in the sense of 'turn out well, have a favorable result' began in the late fifteenth century. We can see from the evolution of this word that success is closely tied to taking action.

In order to experience life to the fullest, we need to choose to take action, even if it can sometimes be challenging or intimidating. Theodore Roosevelt said, "In any moment of decision, the best thing you can do is the right thing, the next best thing is the wrong thing, and the worst thing you can do is nothing." If you make the wrong choice, you still have the chance to grow and learn from your mistakes; if you make no choice, you remain stagnant and learn nothing. Decisions that aren't followed by some kind of action, that don't ignite a change, are simply wasted opportunities. Inaction can leave you with the feelings of regret and the sense that life is something that happens to you, rather than living the life you want.

There are a variety of simple things you can do to start putting "It's Your Decision" into practice. Let's take a look at a few of them:

- ***Share with others what you have learned.*** When you tell others about your decisions, you not only create accountability for yourself, but you also reinforce your choices by saying them out loud. Start by telling your significant other, a close friend, or a trusted colleague. Be mindful that these are individuals you trust, and who you know will support you. Many times, when you tell people about your aspirations, they tend to tell you why what you've decided will not work. This can be a negative drain on your progress towards achieving your goals, so it's important that those you confide in are supportive. Note, if you share your decision with someone who in turn tells you why your decision won't work, sincerely thank them for their input and don't include them in your accountability group going forward. Positive reinforcement is a key ingredient to achieving your dreams and it's important to minimize negative forces as quickly as possible.

- *Write down your decision and put it where you can see it.* Surround yourself with sticky notes at home, or write your decisions on a whiteboard at work. Declare your decisions by posting notes in your car, the bathroom mirror, and even on the refrigerator. If you like to exercise, jog, or walk, you can record your decisions and play them back while you exercise. As is known from the law of attraction, what you focus on expands. You will be reminded of your decision everywhere you go! Each day, you will find renewed inspiration to keep implementing your decisions.

- *Make your decisions part of your daily routine.* If you have decided to hug at least one person a day, take action first thing in the morning, to ensure you don't put it off until late in the day and run the risk of possibly forgetting. When you want to put your decision into action, find a way to build it into your daily routine. Keep track of your progress toward each action step in your decision. If you need some motivation, add it to your To-Do list or calendar and mark it as complete when you follow through with it. Do not move on to the next one until you have mastered the current existing decision.

- *Invite a friend or family member to join you and take action with you.* Not only does accountability help, but you may also find you need support and encouragement. Involve trusted family members and friends in your efforts so they can provide you with reassurance and guidance, if and when you experience challenges. Even better, work together and cheer each other on.

- *Appreciate the knowledge you have gained from putting your decisions into action.* When you maintain the perspective that even mistakes can help you learn and grow, you continuously open yourself up to new opportunities to move forward in life. Don't be afraid to make mistakes, and don't get caught up in worrying about what others think of you—be confident in your decisions, and you will continually learn more about yourself and the world around you.

Be kind to yourself, and give yourself some grace. Change can be scary, even if it's for the better, and it takes time and courage. "It's Your Decision" at its core, aims to give you more control over your life. It is up to you to be the person you want to be, to accept and love who you are, and to step forward into the exciting journey your future holds. If you choose to believe that you have no choice in the matter and live with the mentality that 'whatever happens, happens,' then your life may feel a bit uncertain. Don't gamble with your future, your quality of life is what's at stake. If you believe that you have control over what happens in your life, then you may find that life turns out the way you desire, more often than not.

Those who believe that life is uncertain and holds no guarantees are not completely wrong. But while there can never be any assurances that you will live a perfect life, remember that you can take matters into your own hands when it comes to your attitude, your perspective, and the choices you make. As Mark Twain so wisely said, "Action speaks louder than words, but not nearly as often." The difference between making decisions and putting your decisions into action may be the difference between 'life happens' and 'it's a wonderful life.' It's your decision. Which do you choose?

Chapter 9

Conclusion

Implementing change in your life takes a considerable amount of time and effort, and you have only just begun your journey. It begins with one decision; the decision to stop being a victim of circumstance and take control of your happiness. The decision to create the life you want to live; a life of your own design. You're at the starting line. Make one decision at a time, and then turn those decisions into actions. You have an opportunity to jump right into the heart of your life, instead of standing on the sidelines, watching as life passes you by.

Decide that love is one of humankind's greatest gifts – don't be afraid to love.

The ability to give and receive love is the greatest gift of all. God made us in His image, because of His love. We know that love needs an outlet; love yearns to be expressed and shared with others. When we focus on sharing our love and accepting the love of others, we stay connected to one another and to the world.

Decide to be happy, right now. Make choosing happiness a priority every single day; decide to be loving and happy by simply saying no to unhappiness. While we all have different dreams and life goals, for most of us, living a meaningful life that positively influences others is important. Happiness isn't so much about what you have, because life evolves, your 'blessings' change. You control how you view and interpret your circumstances. Happiness is a choice; choose to concentrate on the good things in your life, and in the world around you.

Decide that 'it' is easy, not hard. Drop your self-imposed limits and stretch yourself right into the dreams you've always had for yourself. Why not consider that anything is possible? Time and again, history has proven that amazing results are born from those who set goals that everyone else thought were unrealistic or impossible. The unattainable and beyond reach are yours for the taking when you decide that 'it' is easy and not hard.

Decide to hug someone today—you 'll make their day and yours! Hugging at its most basic is the world's best-known universal language. It conveys a special kind of communication between two people, without the need for words. The best part of a hug is that you usually can't give one without getting one in return.

Decide to genuinely listen more often than you speak. Be authentic with yourself and others. Be fully present in every moment, by focusing without reservation on the people in your life. Listening attentively can make such a difference in our lives, yet we spend little time developing our listening skills. In our personal lives, listening contributes to helping others feel valued and understood. In our business relationships, taking the time to genuinely listen to others can be a factor in saving time and money, by preventing misunderstandings and clarifying goals.

Decide to be healthy, starting right now. When we decide to make our health a priority, we enhance not only our own personal experiences, but we also plant seeds that can change the lives of others. Whatever the motivator, the outcome is the same—we begin to see that our physical health impacts every aspect of our lives for the better. By deciding to be healthy, this choice becomes more than a goal, it becomes a way of life.

Decide to be the person you want to be, and be that person, starting right now. Decisions bring an action, and action brings change. A single decision can open the door to the life you've always dreamed of living. You are off to a great start by deciding to read this book. Next, take the steps to become who you want to be. The decision is yours.

Call to Action

You made it to the end of the book, and you're probably thinking 'well, now what?' Now is the time for you to take everything you've read and learned in the previous chapters, and put it into action. In my experience, writing something down gives it life - it makes it real.

We spend our lives making promises to other people, and for the most part, we keep them. We show that we have integrity and that our word is good. But when it comes to ourselves, we have a tendency to lack that same principle. This is where you change that. This is your time; the time you're choosing to take for yourself, to forge through your self-imposed obstacles and challenges, and to create the life you've always dreamed of. The time when you start showing yourself the same integrity you show others.

Take the next few pages to write down the promises you're making (and hopefully keeping!) to yourself. Write down your decisions, and the steps you're going to take to reach your goals. If you need help with this exercise, you may find it useful to refer to the Introduction, where I outlined the five steps to successfully achieve your goals. Make sure you refer back to your goals often, checking off the steps when you've accomplished them; perhaps adding new steps, or journaling your victories and challenges along the way.

If you find there isn't enough space here, or if you've purchased the electronic version of this book, you can also go to www.itsyourdecisiontoday.com.

Now, make your decisions, follow the steps, and change your life.

_____

_____

_____

_____

_____

_____

_____

_____

_____

_____

_____

_____

_____

_____

_____

_____

_____

_____

Dr. Milton Mattox

94

_____
_____
_____
_____
_____
_____
_____
_____
_____
_____
_____
_____
_____
_____
_____
_____
_____
_____
_____
_____
_____
_____
_____
_____
_____
_____
_____
_____
_____

Dr. Milton Mattox

www.ingramcontent.com/pod-product-compliance
Lightning Source LLC
Chambersburg PA
CBHW032116280326
41933CB00009B/861